Transport in Asia

Lisa James

Contents

Transport

In Asia, there are many ways to get from one place to another.

Some are slow and some are fast.

Let's take a look at some of the most interesting ways of getting around in Asia.

train

Map of Asia

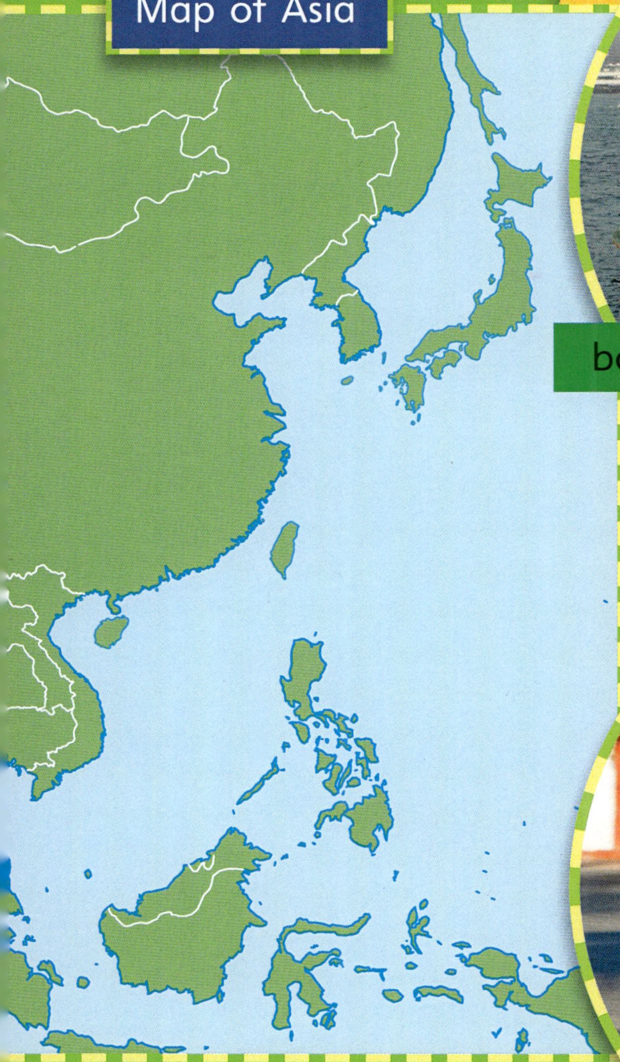

boat

bike

rickshaw

Bikes

A lot of people ride bikes in Asia.
It is a quick way to go from place to place.
The **bike lanes** are very wide in the cities.

Some bikes carry a lot of things!

Rickshaws

A **rickshaw** is a small cart.
It carries people or things from place to place.
Some rickshaws have two wheels.
They are pulled by people.

Some rickshaws have motors.
They are small and move quickly!

Boats

This boat is called a **ferry**.
Ferries take people over the water.
They can take lots of people.

This boat is called a **slow boat**.
It takes a long time to go down the river.

Trains

Some trains go under the ground.
They carry lots of people every day.
They are a fast way to travel.

Some places in Asia have hundreds of train tracks under the ground.

Here is a map of some underground train lines.

Some trains go high above the ground.
They are called **sky trains**.

Sky trains can go over rivers and lakes.

Some trains go in a straight line.
They do not have to slow down for corners.
They are called **bullet trains**.

Bullet trains are very fast!

Glossary

bike lanes special lanes on the road that are just for bicycles

bullet trains very fast trains that travel on flat tracks

ferry a type of boat that takes people or goods over short distances

rickshaw a small vehicle that can only take one or two people at a time

sky trains trains that run on rails, high up in the air

slow boat a large boat that moves very slowly